Mom & Dad,

Tell Me
About Your Life

Precious memories,
invaluable wisdom and
personal experience
for your children

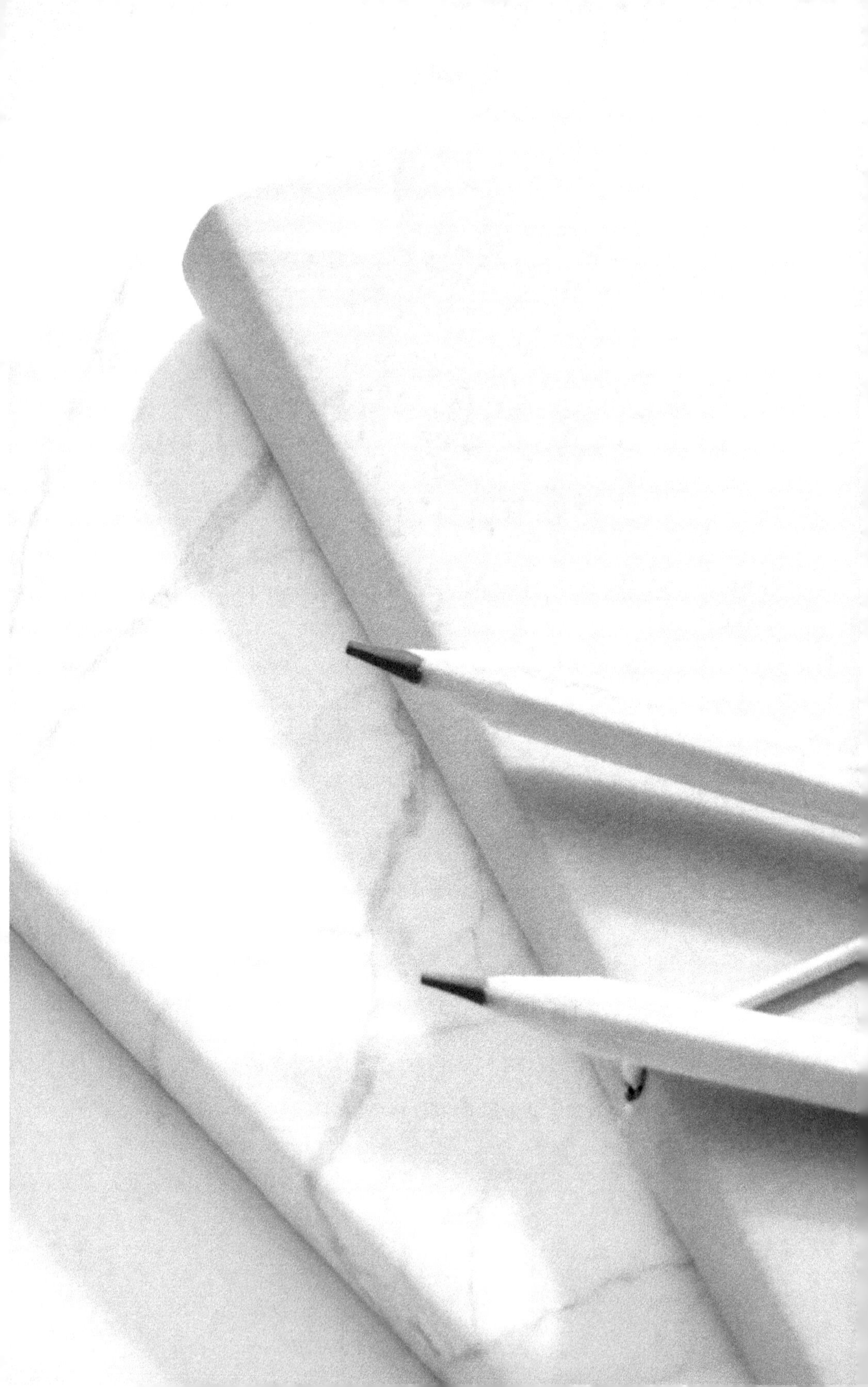

Dear Mom, dear Dad!

You have already experienced a lot. Did great things, had a lot of fun and went through thick and thin together.

With all the lightness and joy you have always increased in wisdom, gathered experiences and have been profoundly shaped.

Of course, there were also moments in your life when the warm sunlight hid behind dark clouds. Where you were not so well.

All these stories and experiences from life are a precious treasure for your children.

It would be too bad if we never heard this abundance of stories and happenings.

Also, you surely have a lot of advice and recommendations how we can behave optimally in different circumstances.

We want you to take the time to look at your life.

With this book you get a selection of far-reaching questions that you can answer. Your answers will enrich us and give us even more insights into your life.

We hope you enjoy the writing!

With great love,

Childhood

Childhood

Mom as
a child

Dad as
a child

Childhood

How did your parents find each other?

Under what circumstances did your birth take place?

Do your first names have a deeper meaning?

Childhood

Are you happy with your first names?

Do you have siblings?

How was the relationship and harmony in your family?

Childhood

Do you have nicknames?

> "Every child is an artist. The problem is how to remain an artist once we grow up."

Pablo Picasso

What's the first thing that comes to mind when you think of your childhood?

Childhood

What made your kids' eyes light up?

Were you rich?

What was the house/apartment like where you grew up?

Childhood

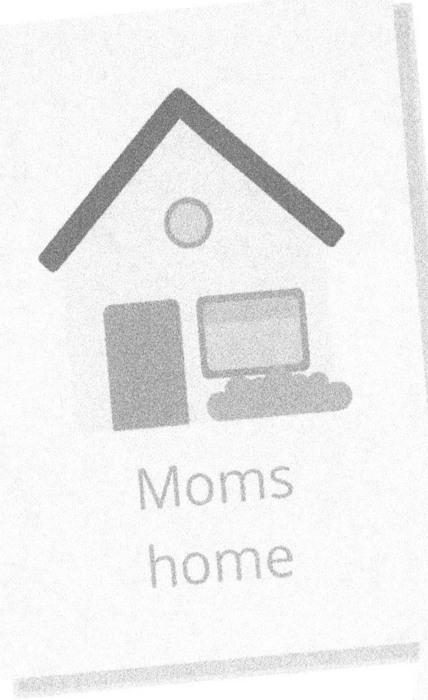

What neighborhood did you live in?

How did you learn to ride a bike?

How did you do in school?

Childhood

Do you still have childhood friends today?

What stories did you like to hear?

Did you have animals?

What profession did you dream of at that time?

"The soul is healed by being
with children."

Fyodor Dostoevsky

Where did you go most often on vacation?

Childhood

What was your favorite dish that your parents/grandparents made?

Did you get hurt as a child? How did it happen?

What impactful or drastic life experience did you have as a child?

Childhood

Did you have fears? Do they still exist today?

What activity as a child would you still like to do today?

Favorite games
as a child

01 ....

02 ....

03 ....

04 ....

05 ....

Childhood

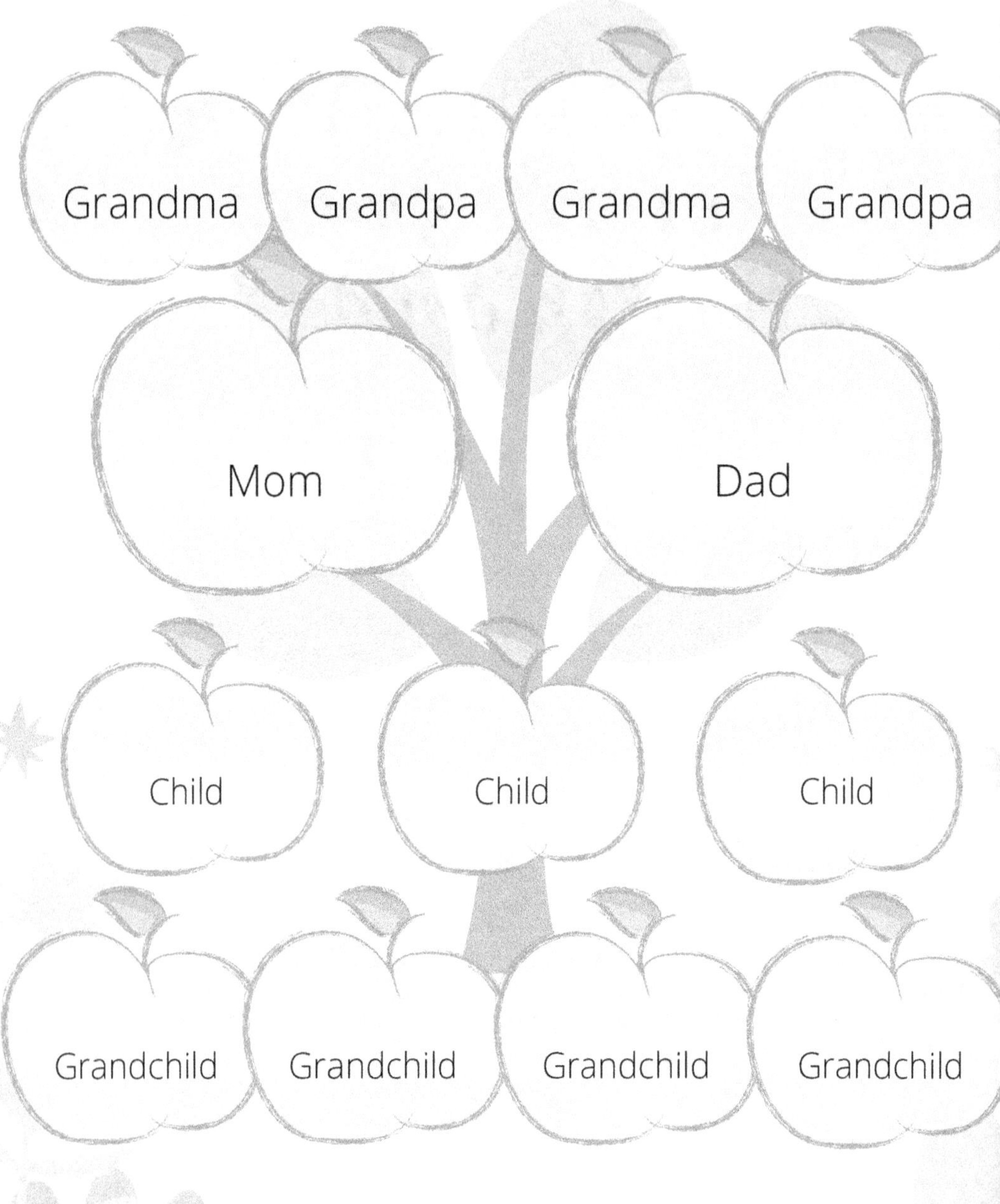

Grandma
Grandpa
Grandma
Grandpa
Mom
Dad
Child
Child
Child
Grandchild
Grandchild
Grandchild
Grandchild

Puberty

Puberty

Puberty

How did you dress?

Do you have a special characteristic of your body that makes you stand out?

Do you look more like your mother or father?

What memory from your youth still brings you laughter today?

What problems did you have to deal with?

What characteristics of your parents were you determined *not* to adopt?

Puberty

What was your attitude towards the teachers like?

> **"Puberty is a potpourri of emotions."**
>
> Marina Zuber

Did you enjoy going to school?

Puberty

Have you committed any crimes?

What political/cultural events took place when you were a teen?

Which stars did you admire?

Puberty

What did you learn in class that you remember very well
today?

What did you think about old people?

What was the craziest thing you did as a teenager?

What were your best vacations as a teenager?

"**Youth is the gift of nature,
but age is a work of art.**"

Stanislaw Jerzy
Lec

What terribly embarrassing thing happened to you?

Puberty

Were you envious of the lives of others around you?

What hobbies did you have?

Have you participated in any contests?

THAT SHAPED OUR
GENERATION

1

2

3

4

5

6

7

8

9

10

Adulthood

Mom as
an adult

Dad as
an adult

Why I'm so grateful to have you two:

I have a great example to follow. You!

You always have the right words to make everything more pleasant.

Nothing is better than the love of parents, and the same can be said about you.

You give the most amazing hugs!

You are the most wonderful Mom & Dad in this world!

Adulthood

What did you love to do as adults?

What are you grateful for?

Does a song have a special meaning for you?

Adulthood

Have you taken to the streets for social interests?

What is the best compliment you have received?

What was your first car?

Your first car

Adulthood

What approach to finances have you cultivated?

"Yesterday is history,
tomorrow is a mystery,
today is a gift of God,
which is why we call it the
present."

Bil Keane

What was your biggest bad buy?

Adulthood

How resilient were you under stress?

How did you two meet?

When did you move in together?

Adulthood

Adulthood

From Dad: "What I appreciate about Mom"

Adulthood

How was your wedding?

Do any of you snore?

At what age did you become parents?

To Mom: What was it like for you to be pregnant?

> **"There shall be an eternal summer in the grateful heart."**
>
> Celia Thaxter

How did you choose your children's names?

Adulthood

Where did you learn about raising children?

What is the most wonderful thing about being a parent?

How has being a parent shaped you personally?

Adulthood

What outrageous things did your children do?

What were the funniest things your children did?

Which of your children's first words can you remember?

Adulthood

What are you proud of regarding your children?

Have you traveled a lot? Tell me about your most beautiful journey together!

Have you met any famous people?

Adulthood

Important cities for us:

Important countries for us:

What unexplainable phenomena / supernatural miracles have you experienced?

What makes you smile?

What important life wisdom would you share with your "18-year-old self"?

TOP 10
mistakes to avoid

1

2

3

4

5

6

7

8

9

10

*He achieved success who has lived well,
laughed often, and loved much;*

*Who has enjoyed the trust of pure women,
the respect of intelligent men and
the love of little children;*

Who has filled his niche and accomplished his task;

*Who has never lacked appreciation of Earth's beauty
or failed to express it;*

*Who has left the world better than he found it,
Whether an improved poppy, a perfect poem,
or a rescued soul;*

*Who has always looked for the best in others and
given them the best he had;*

Whose life was an inspiration;

Whose memory a benediction.

Bessie Anderson Stanley, 1897-1952

Higher
Age

Mom
today

Dad
today

Higher Age

How did you get to your current house/apartment?

What are you most looking forward to about (future) retirement?

Is it hard to get older?

Higher Age

Do you regret (not) doing something?

Do you have a "skeleton in the closet"?

What do you do all day long?

WELLNESS-DAY

Choose an activity for your self-care and have a feel-good day.

What topics do you like to talk about?

> "Age does not protect you from love, but love protects you from age."

Jeanne Moreau

What would your perfect day look like?

Higher Age

What is the best memory of your life as a couple so far?

How do you look at youth now?

What do you not dare to tell the children personally in
conversation?

Higher Age

If you had one wish: What would you wish for?

Do you feel lonely?

What has your opinion changed radically compared to before?

OUR FAVORITE PRODUCTS IN THE SUPERMARKET:

Higher Age

How has your character changed?

What would you rescue from a burning house?

Are you afraid of dying?

THINGS THAT YOU UNDERSTAND WHEN YOU'RE OLDER

Staying at home is also fun	Things will develop as they should	Relationships are everything	It's perfectly ok, to be vulnerable	pay bills on time
"I should have saved more money!"	Work is not everything	Visit the family more often	Always trust your intuition	Success does not happen overnight
Efforts are part of life	There is always something new to learn about life	Don't take it so seriously	Getting out of your comfort zone is important	There are no ordinary Moments
Better late than never	Relax more often	To realize the desired life is beautiful	Health is wealth	You are never too old to learn something new
Time heals all wounds	Thank people more	Talking is the best therapy	Your mistakes do not define you	8 hours of sleep is pure bliss

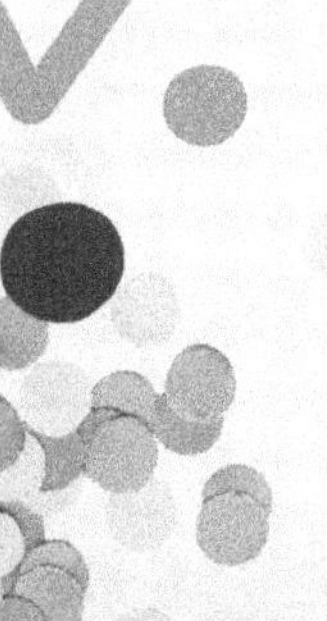
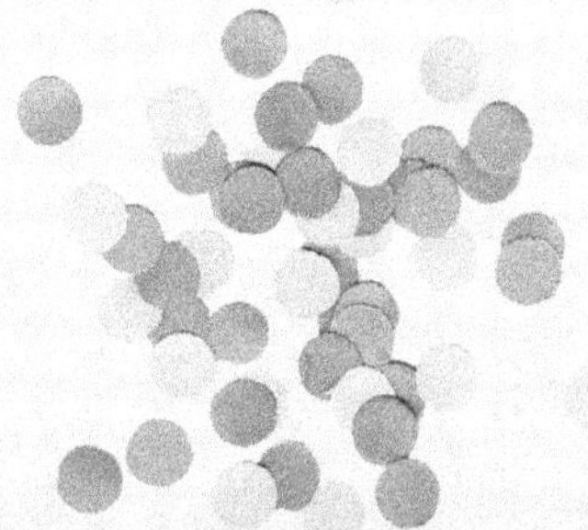

Do you believe in life after death?

If you believe in it: How do you get to heaven?

What are your aspirations for your funeral?

Does a certain smell evoke intense memories in you?

"Gray hair is a crown of
splendor;
it is attained in the way
of righteousness."

Proverbs 16:31

Do you want to move/emigrate?

Higher Age

What goals and dreams do you have for the future?

Was everything better in the past?

What moments in life are you especially happy about?

Higher Age

From which life crisis did you emerge stronger?

Which people have helped you in a special way?

What important experiences would you like to share?

What can I do to delight you?

How do you imagine the world in 2050?

What is your life so far in one sentence?

Goals for the future

For my parents!

These lines are for you -
for my parents, whom I love.

You took care of me for years,
but did rarely hear how much you mean to me.
I would therefore like to take this opportunity to say
thank you.

You have helped me from the beginning,
when I took the first, wobbly steps and
are still there for me today, when I fall down some time.

Thank you for letting me go a little more with each step,
so I could learn to stand on my own two feet.
Thank you that I could always feel safe with you.
Thank you for the love I could always be sure of.

Thank you for the many years in which you have never
stopped
to care for me and in whom you have tried everything,
to turn my dreams into successes.

Thank you for your patience and understanding,
That you gave me when I went my own way.
Thank you for your love, without which I could not have lived.
Thank you for everything you have done and are still doing for
me!

With your love and experience you have made me that person,
who I am today.

Hopefully I will be able to give my children
as much as you've given to me.

Relationships

Relationships

What do you admire about your parents?

What caused conflicts with your parents?

Is there love at first sight?

Relationships

How did you overcome the first heartbreak?

How did you know mom/dad was the one?

What are the requirements for marriage?

How to get along with the in-laws?

"Darkness cannot drive out darkness; only light can do that. Hate cannot drive out hate; only love can do that."

Martin Luther King, Jr.

Can you remember your first dispute?

Relationships

What advice do you have for a beautiful marriage?

How do you find the relationship today in our family?

What advice do you have for successful parenting?

Pet names to mom

Pet names to dad

Relationships

What attributes of people make you angry?

How do you learn forgiveness?

How do you deal with criticism?

When was the last time you said "I love you!" to someone?

"A drop of love is more than an ocean of knowledge."

Blaise Pascal

What do you appreciate most about other people?

Why do others seek your presence?

What puts others off from you?

Who are your friends today?

Relationships

How have you dealt with bereavement?

How do you want others to remember you?

How do you define love?

TOP 10 RULES
Dealing with people

1

2

3

4

5

6

7

8

9

10

Career

Career

Should there be mandatory community service?

What vocational training/studies have you completed?

What was/is your favorite job?

Career

What kind of work can you not stand at all?

Have you ever failed with your own business?

Which of your work activities would you do without pay?

How do you make decisions?

> "I can't change the
> direction of the wind, but I
> can adjust my sails to
> always reach my
> destination."

Jimmy Dean

How to find the dream job?

DO YOU HAVE SLEEP PROBLEMS?

1. No distractions in your room

2. No coffee or sweet drinks 5 hours before bedtime

3. Exercise regularly

4. Too many thoughts? Write them down in a journal.

5. If you can't sleep, don't force it.

6. If your lack of sleep is affecting your daily life, consult a doctor.

Career

Which boss do you think back to with favor?

Have you found the meaning of life after all these years?

For which problem of mankind would you like to have a solution?

Career

What topic would you like to write a book about?

Whose heroic work would you like to have made?
(Example: Martin Luther King, Jr.)

What superhero power would you like to have?

Message to the world:

Do you do any volunteer work?

"Pleasure in the job puts perfection in the work."

Aristotle

For which organization / project could I donate?

Tips for career success

01 ....

02 ....

03 ....

04 ....

05 ....

Miscellaneous

Which do you prefer?

(Please mark: Mom's color | Dad's color)

City trip	Beach
Relaxed	Nervous
Save	Waste
Meat	Vegetables
Stubborn	Harmonious
Vanilla	Chocolate
Comedy	Action
Elevator	Stairs
Classic	Hip Hop
Cinema	Couch

Which do you prefer?

Jogging	Volleyball
Family	Career
Introvert	Extrovert
Summer	Winter
Conscientious	Sloppy
Coffee	Tea
Conservative	Liberal
Left	Right
Sleep in	Early Bird
Dog	Cat

Which do you prefer?

Pajamas	Tuxedo
Garden	Roof terrace
Flying	Taking a train
Optimistic	Pessimistic
Party	Chilling
Nutella	Honey
Teamwork	Alone
Sweden	Spain
Farm	Villa
Email	Call

Which do you prefer?

Whole milk	Bittersweet
Inside young	Old & wise
Cooking	Delivery service
Swimming pool	Lake
Colorful	Grey
Apple	Samsung
Long hair	Short hair
Bicycle	Car
Heart	Head
Slippers	High Heels

This or that

Which do you prefer?

Makeup	Nature
Kitchen	Living room
World hunger	Climate change
Sweet	Salty
Watching sports	Doing sports
Cash	Bitcoin
Flea Market	Shopping Mall
Home Office	Business Trip
Economics	Philosophy
YouTube	Podcast

This or that

Which do you prefer?

Freezing	Sweating
1900	2100
Rice	Noodles
Amazon	Kiosk
Chess	Uno
Sun	Moon
Paperback	eBook
Money	Fame
Office	Garage
Gifts	Compliments

TOP 10
Wisdoms of life

1

2

3

4

5

6

7

8

9

10

Favorite books

01 ....

02 ....

03 ....

04 ....

05 ....

Our favorite spots

Favorite words

1

2

3

4

5

6

7

8

9

10

Favorite websites

Own questions

Own questions

Own questions

Family recipe

NAME: TIME: SERVINGS:

Ingredients

Preparation

Family recipe

NAME: TIME: SERVINGS:

Ingredients

Preparation

Family recipe

NAME: TIME: SERVINGS:

Ingredients

Preparation

Letter from mom

Letter from dad

Space for other content

Space for other content

Space for other content

Space for other content

www.ingramcontent.com/pod-product-compliance
Lightning Source LLC
LaVergne TN
LVHW010233200726

843506LV00014B/2975